www.islington.gov.uk

 ISLINGTON

T 020 7527 6900

Islington Libraries

1 5 FEB 2019

01|19

Please return this item on or before the last date stamped below or you may be liable to overdue charges.

To renew an item call the number below, or access the on-line catalogue at www.islington.gov.uk/libraries

You will need your library membership number and PIN number.

Let's hear it for Humbug!

For all individuals, especially Mand! – Mike
For the wild, the wise and the woolly! – Deborah

A Templar Book

First published in the UK in 2001 by Templar Publishing,
an imprint of The Templar Company plc,
Pippbrook Mill, London Road, Dorking, Surrey, RH4 1JE, UK
www.templarco.co.uk

Distributed in the UK by Ragged Bears Ltd.,
Ragged Appleshaw, Andover, Hampshire, SP11 9HX

ISBN 1-84011-097-X

Design by Mike Jolley
All-singing-all-dancing pop by Richard Hawke
Words tweaked by Dugald Steer

Printed with ink on a big machine in China

If you have enjoyed this book, then tell all your friends,
and look for our other book called **'Grunter** – the story of a pig with attitude!'
If you haven't, then keep quiet!
(But remember to make up your own mind)

Baa Humbug!

A sheep with a mind of his own

words by **mike jolley**

pictures by **deborah allwright**

templar publishing

All sheep are

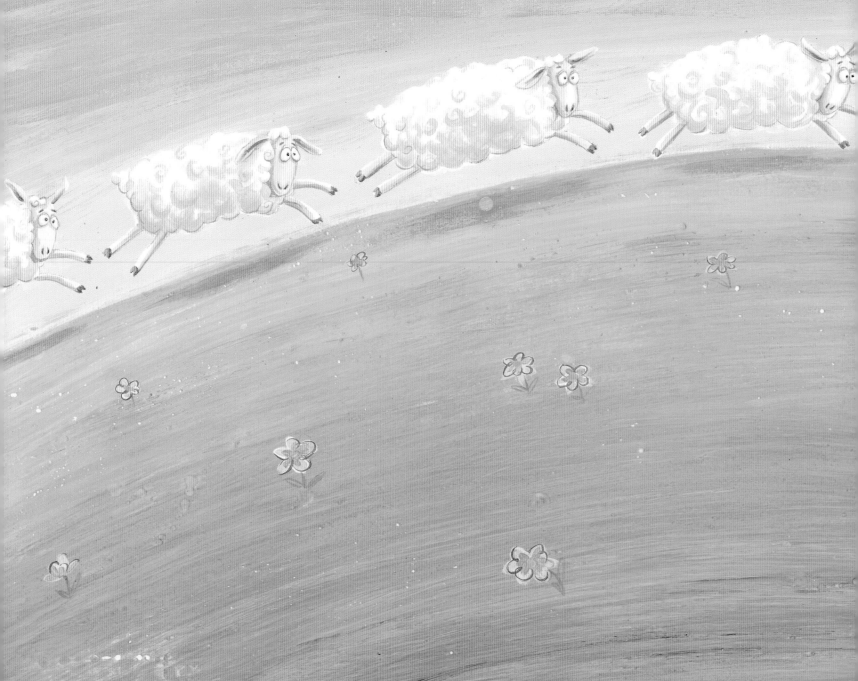

stupid.

Or so you may think…

But this is the story of a different sheep.
A sheep with a mind of his own.

A **unique** sheep.

A sheep called Humbug!

'Tra-la!' said Humbug,
doing a trick for the fun of it.

'You can't say tra-la,
you have to say baa,'
said the other sheep.

'Baa! Baa!

because that's what
sheep do!'

Hoorah!

'Hogwash!'

said Humbug,

and then he said 'Moo!'

(which, after all, was a fun thing to do!)

When it rained, the sheep huddled in the shed.
But, guess what? Humbug did not!
'Don't you think that your wool will shrink?'
worried the sheep.
'Think! Shrink!'

Think! Shrink!'

'Rubbish!'

said Humbug,

and he danced the fandango!

(then a twist and a tango!)

'You'll look the farm fool
if you don't cut your wool!' said the sheep
on shearing day. 'Fool!
Wool!

'Piffle!'
said Humbug.

'Wool is for wearing!'

(not shearing and sharing!)

'The dip may be cold
but it's healthy we're told!'
bleated the sheep as they shivered
in the frosty field.

'It's cold
we're told!
Cold we're
told!'

'**Humbug!**' said Humbug,

But –
when the sheep said,
'Here comes the man,
we must go in the van.'

'Man! Van!

Man! Van!'

Humbug *knew*
just what he had to do...

'Stop!

Think lamb chop!' he said.

...and with the van **key** he set them all *free!*

Free!

Free!

Free!

Free!